NARRATIVES UNSEEN

A COLLECTION OF INVISIBLE INKINGS

RIYANKA PAUL

Made with ♥ on the Notion Press Platform
www.notionpress.com

To my Family,

Mom, Dad, Sister, and family

for their unmatched support of poetry

and

To all the imaginative characters

in my mind, who is a part of

Narratives Unseen.

.

Contents

Contents

Contents

Narratives Unseen

A Collection Of Invisible Inkings

By

Riyanka Paul

Preface

Dear Reader,

Currently, I am fifteen. Within these pages, I weave my soul into every verse. Each line, poured from my heart to my fingertips, carries the weight of emotions—joy, grief, and the ethereal dance of fantasy. I began this poetic journey at the tender age of nine when ink became my closest confidante. But, those poems are not for publishing purposes as they are too childish (in my point of view). Well to tell you a secret, a few of these poems were also not meant for publishing as they were just to give myself a sense of peace and satisfaction about my writing. But something struck me, most probably a 'poetic current', and I decided to publish it because I felt that it needed a different point of view from you, the readers. I always appreciate having one's perspective about a poem.

Fantasy is my muse. It dances through my veins, pirouetting across the parchment. When emotions strike like lightning, I wield my pen as both a sword and a wand. In moments of grief, ink spills like tears, etching pain into stanzas. When delight blooms, verses burst forth like sunflowers reaching for the sun. And in the quiet hours of romance, my words become whispered promises, secret rendezvous between heartbeats.

But I am more than a storyteller; I am an architect of characters. The figures that populate these poems are not mere ink on paper; they are incarnations of longing—the friends I wish to have, the lovers I ache for, the companions who would walk beside me through life's labyrinth.

Nature, too, dances within these lines. I romanticize every dew-kissed leaf, every moonlit meadow, and every breeze that carries whispers from distant hills. Through my eyes, the earth is both a sanctuary and confidante—a place where secrets are shared between roots and stars.

And when love intertwines with life, let it be intrigued. My heart is a compass, ever seeking connections, ever yearning for the touch of another soul. I invite you, dear reader, to step into my world, to read not just with your eyes but with your heart. Interpret, reimagine, and find your reflections in these verses.

So turn the page, and let the ink-stained magic unfold. May you discover your narratives hidden within these lines, and may the characters you meet become old friends, whispering their secrets to you as well.

With unbound love and poisoned ink,

Riyanka Paul

The Poet

P.S. To the characters who dwell here: You are immortal now, etched into eternity by my hand. May your stories resonate in the hearts of readers, forever Narratives Unseen.

Writer's Contact information: contact.riyanka44@gmail.com

Acknowledgements

My Poisoned Pen,

and

My Unbound Heart

Contents Classified

The Dame of time

1. Part I

They say you're getting older,
But, for me, you're getting magnificent with age.
The poets say if you were in my place,
You would've earned twice my wage.

2. Part II

You gazed at the autumn-fall,
And fell like the leaves of them.
You watched my youth,
Shattering and healing
In the best way, it can.

• 5 •

3. Part III

Now I write this elegy,
Sitting hollow-eyed at,
The tombstone of my confidant;
A female Aristocrat.

RIYANKA PAUL

Clare

4. Part I

Clare, I know you,
crooning in the garden,

Watering the plants,
with the tears of your eyes.

Dancing with you,
in those days was golden,

Under the purple, yellow skies.

5. Part II

Clare, I know you,
expostulating with the toughest,
Giving a damn to all the philistines.
With your gleaming hair, covered with stardust,
And your name on the cover page of the magazines.

6. Part III

Even so, it was unknown to me,
That it was a mere folklore.
The flowers on your crimson hat,
Are now wilting near the shore.

7. Part IV

And no one can ever lose you,
'Cause you never lose the one who does not belong to you.
It was forgotten that you have wings, too.

8. Part V

Your wristlets,
And the skirts that you wear;
The glint in your eyes,
And the bow in the hair,
are still lying in the
broken wooden chair.

9. Part VII

Your cut-off wings and a plaintive smile-
Your autumn dreams seem to be afraid.
Did you come to me with regret or doubt,
for the nuisances that we made?

10. Part VIII

Now I gaze at the pictures,
Where we used to sojourn in dreamland.
Now I goggle at the glimmers,
With your melodies imprinted on my nightstand.

Road to Heaven

11. Part I

Once, she asked me if I ever wanted-
"Yes" if I had shouted.
She wouldn't leave me till the end, I suppose.
Leaving the thorn, departed to the rose.

12. Part II

She is a beautiful soul,
Shining, sparkling, wilting, ceasing-
Ceasing on the flame gold,
Flowing to where I reach.

13. Part III

It's never too late, she exclaimed.
Surprisingly, she flies away.
And took my peace as
She went to the godly heaven.

14. Part IV

Never have I ever seen it,
Or Ever tried to feel it.

It's so heavenly out there;
Quietude everywhere.

15. Part V

Heaven is the earth,
Where Rosé lived.
She had none to betray;
Yet also kept the place untouched, even today.

An Elegy For Her

16. Part I

Where whispering willows weep by the stream,
Sunlight strains through leaves in a mournful gleam,
A melody of memories gently I weave,
An elegy for the one I could not keep.

17. Part II

Golden threads woven by her
are the memories we made in an Alcott.
The Alcott possesses a vacant chair now,
for the one residing in 'forever'.

18. Part III

Her beauty may fade,
But, the quintessence remains
In the hearts of her allies.
But her deep sleep still steals the sleep of
The one she was loved by.

Too Old Now

19. Part 1

For that moment,
I would go to heaven and come back,
With tears falling down my
Wrinkled blue eyes.

20. Part II

The time of amenities; the shades of clarity,
flash behind the back of my mind.
The tree grew older but,
Young remained the sunshine.

21. Part III

I saw the oak trees shedding its leaves,
But flourish and grow in the spring.
I saw water falling down the Fall,
And disappearing in front of my eyeball.

22. Part IV

Those Shiny eyes looking into mine,
The tormented face turned into a smile.
The bond aligned with lights in the shadow;
Still cherished in the lone meadow.

23. Part V

I regret the freedom,
That I had lost for
the one who spins a yarn

I yearn to recapture it somehow,
But sorry for ourselves;
We are too old now.

An Astrophil

24. Part I

After all the comets died,
I was redeemed by an archer.
Lost in the ominous fire,
I fear if I am alive.

25. Part II

When I gaze at the twin stars.
All it had to say was "goodbye".

I would spend my entire life stargazing
If only I lived, though.

26. Part III

Love is such a beautiful chaos,
No, I wasn't ever its ally;
Earth signs tell me to grow,
Oh! How adamant I am?

27. Part IV

Now, I stand and stare at
The inner sky.
None of the stars are visible,
Only the desolated dark.

I Think We're in The UK

28. Part I

I sit on the oldest railway,
with a cup of tea and a bill to pay.
Environs seem to be unalike-
I surmise that it is the UK.

29. Part II

The air has got us somewhere-
-where times are real fast,
and varying like the colors of agate
Faith rules yet, decisions do not last.

30. Part III

Perhaps I am laying it on thick,
but there is a method to my madness;
I sought for an idyllic shelter,
seems the hunt is over now.

The Final Sunset?

31. Part I

The final shot was,
As fair as that last one.
Your trigger echoes,
Down deep into my heart.

32. Part II

Marksmen's lament
reflected a sense of relief,
prior to this
was someone screaming?

In the shades of dark,
when the truth was hidden.
We searched with hearts alight,
a secret fire kindled.

33. Part III

Would our sunset, paint the world's last light?
Aren't there more like us, burning bright?

There are, and the flames will ignite,
Though embers may fade in the fading night.

Dear Poppy,

34. Part I

Dear Poppy,
I poured life into you,
At fifteen, while you were two.
Your silence brought tranquility
when I was misconstrued.

35. Part II

Now, your papery petals grace my grave,
I don't see it, for I am asleep.
But, I sense a quiet assurance,
Along with a warm crimson blanket.

36. Part III

Under the nightfall, I'd whisper:
"Your crimson complemented my blood."
Your curtains covered my garden,
like how you veil me now,
But with a poignant difference.

The White Palace

37. Part I

A sorceress table placed in the middle
of a canvas white, against the emerald wood.
Magic wands, scattered in and around;
I'll take you to the place where they once settled.

38. Part II

The folks of grandiose;
Their sons and daughters, With silver spoons and sapphires.
A palace born of dreams, of gilded halls,
Now echoes whisper of forgotten calls.

39. Part III

Those curtains of faded white,
This remembrance is never light.
A silent sentinel, it stands alone,
A ghostly relic now sits on history's throne.

40. Part IV

No longer echoes of delight reside,
Just mournful whispers where once joy did abide.
A ghost of splendor, where sorrow now does dwell,
The White Palace weeps, a fading, mournful spell.

This is not

The End

Riyanka Paul